An Introduction
to
New Testament
Greek

A Crash Course in Koine Greek for Homeschoolers and the Self-Taught

by
Dr. Anthony Horvath

An Introduction to New Testament Greek
  A Crash Course in Koine Greek for Homeschoolers and the Self-Taught

  By Dr. Anthony Horvath

Soft Cover: ISBN 978-1-947844-62-9   [This edition.]
Hard Cover: ISBN: 978-1-64594-043-2

This book can be purchased as a PDF download, allowing for easy printing of worksheets and resources, via the Athanatos Publishing website:

www.athanatos.org

NOTE:

An Introduction to New Testament Greek

A Crash Course in Koine Greek for Homeschoolers and the Self-Taught

Take your Bible Studies to the next level.

Biblical Greek Study Course

- Objective: Upon the completion of this program the participant will be able to determine what the Greek words are behind the English translation and then determine what those words mean using reference works such as lexicons and interlinears.
- Approximate duration: 3 to 6 weeks.
- Age of Participants: *Some* 7th graders and Up.

Contents

Unit 1

Unit 2

Biblical Greek in A *Flash*

Unit 1

Who is this for? Those wishing to teach Greek… teachers, parents, homeschoolers, pastors, youth directors
What will be learned? Enough Greek to open up the New Testament and look up the words they find
Who will benefit? Anyone wanting to take their study of the Bible to the next level!

"It's all Greek to me!" goes the saying. In fact, Greek is not a difficult language to learn. That is good news for Christians because they know that the New Testament is all in Greek. People know when they read their English translation that sometimes the original Greek had more meaning or nuance than was possible to render in the English. For many, however, the original text is utterly inaccessible. At best, they have to rely on the statements of others.

The purpose of this program is to provide the essential knowledge that will allow people to access the Greek New Testament. The purpose of this program is not to equip people with the ability to translate the text for themselves. The goal is to give them enough of the basics so that they can investigate the original Greek text. At the end of this program, students will:

- know the Greek alphabet
- be able to recognize and distinguish between nouns and verbs
- be able to navigate a Greek New Testament
- be able to look up Greek words in a Greek lexicon
- have a basic foundation for further study of the Greek language.

How long will it take?

Not as long as you might think! One can complete it in three weeks by taking a lesson a week or one can extend it by doing extra practice on lessons that posed difficulty and finish in about six weeks.

In Unit 2, vocabulary is added, definite pronouns and adjectives are covered, and more interaction with research tools is provided.

How old should the learner be?

The techniques used in Unit 1 have been employed with students as early as 7th grade. It depends largely on the capabilities of the learner. Portions of this unit rely on the Internet and in this day and age, 7th graders are more than able to handle such websites.

What do you mean, "enough Greek to be dangerous"?

There are two ways this phrase can be taken. In the first place, it playfully suggests that with this new understanding of Greek, you'll be able to slay ignorance. In the second place, there is a more serious aspect, which the learner would do well to remember: this book is not going to make you thoroughly conversant in Biblical Greek. You will *not* be a Bible translator. There will be tons you still do not know, and so any conclusions you draw from your access to the Greek at this level must be held tentatively and humbly. It could be dangerous to your own soul, or those of others. You are warned.

Lesson One

Learning the Language

The bedrock of a language is its alphabet. Many languages today use the same letters—the Roman alphabet. It is more complicated to learn Greek and Hebrew because they use a completely different lettering. Fortunately, since the Roman alphabet evolved from the Greek alphabet, there are enough similarities that learning the letters isn't as hard as it might seem.

In this lesson, we will learn the letters of the Greek alphabet.

In order to learn the alphabet we are going to have the students *transliterate*. Transliteration is taking the words from one language and using the letters of another language to re-create the sound of that word. We will be taking English words and re-creating them using Greek letters. Because the words are English words, students need not be intimidated at the prospect of trying to sound out Greek words they don't know the meaning of.

So, for example, let's take the English word 'cat.' Using the alphabet chart provided (Resource One) to identify which Greek letters can re-create this word. The correct answer would be:

κατ

Another example might be the word 'fate.' In this case, though in the English we still use the 'a', in the Greek there is a letter of the alphabet dedicated to the long 'a' sound, the Eta: η. So, keeping in mind that the 'e' is silent, the correct answer would be:

φητ

Repeat the exercises in this lesson until it seems that the students have grasped the alphabet. It shouldn't take very long. See lesson six for information on the 'h' and 'ng' sounds.

It is easy to practice transliteration if you have access to a computer word processing program. **You can take any English text, highlight it, and change the font to the 'symbol' font, which in Microsoft Word is the Greek letter font.** Note that you may have to 'clean' up the text because English has silent letters and the Greek forms some sounds differently, like for example using two letters to make two sounds that the English accomplishes in one letter (like the English letter 'a' accomplishing the work of both the Eta and Alpha).

Having students actually write out their English words using Greek letters has the benefit of making them think through the process in a different way than simply changing the font. Optionally, then, you can request that students handwrite the exercises rather than complete them on a word processor.

Accents and Breathing Marks

Though Greek uses accent marks constantly, at the level of Greek you'll end up with after this document, they will rarely matter that much to you one way or another. Almost all of the Greek words in this document also had accent marks, but in general, we will set aside accents.

Greek also has breathing marks. These little marks hover over letters and tell you that you need to add an 'h' sound. The biggest example we will come into contact with is the definite article ov. We will cover definite articles in Unit Two.

If you carefully look at a passage where there is a definite article, you will see a little mark above it. ον is pronounced "hon."

Other words have breathing marks, too.

The Double Gamma

Finally, as far as pronunciation goes, it may have been noticed that sometimes the Greek puts two gammas (γγ) together. The English rarely does this but we already use the same sound. The best example from the New Testament is the word αγγελλος. This word is *not* pronounced 'ag-gel-los'! This Greek word is where we get our word 'angel.' The English pronunciation of the 'g' in this instance is hard, as in 'jet', but in the Greek the 'g' sound when there is a double gamma is soft, as in 'get.' The pronunciation, therefore, is 'angelo.' However, this word also has a breathing mark, so really its 'hangelos'!

When you see a double gamma, make a 'ng' sound, as in runn**ing** or a**ng**el.

Distribute Resource One providing the charts comparing nouns and verbs and explain:

1. The difference between *translating* and *transliterating*.
2. The Greek alphabet is very similar to the English one but there are differences that should be noted.
3. What some of those differences are (eg, 2 Greek vowels for 1 English one).
4. Accents are occasionally important for determining word meaning.
5. Breathing marks are occasionally important for determining word pronunciation and make the 'h' sound.
6. That two gammas together, in the Greek, make the 'ng' sound.

Note: while there are some manuscripts that come to us in upper case alphabetic letters, most are in lower case. New Testaments in Greek that you can purchase today are almost completely in lower case, so we will spend no time on the upper case.

Greek Alphabet Table
Resource One

Greek Letter	Name	Sound letter, as in…	Letter on Keyboard
α	Alpha	a, father	a
β	Beta	b, boy	b
γ	Gamma	g, got	g
δ	Delta	d, dog	d
ε	Epsilon	e, bet	e
ζ	Zeta	dz, suds	z
η	Eta	a, hay	h
θ	Theta	th, think	q
ι	Iota	i, sit	i
κ	Kappa	k, kitchen	k
λ	Lambda	l, look	l
μ	Mu	m, move	m
ν	Nu	n, not	n
ξ	Xi	x, axe	x
ο	Omicron	o, ought	o
π	Pi	p, pea	p
ρ	Rho	r, are	r
σ/ς	Sigma	s, sing	s/V (shift-v)
τ	Tau	t, town	t
υ	Upsilon	u, moon	u
φ	Phi	ph, fig	f
χ	Chi	ch, christen	c
ψ	Psi	ps, hips	y
ω	Omega	o, note	w
Note: the ς is used when the sigma comes at the end of the word.			

Short vowels: ε , ο

Long vowels: η , ω

Variable vowels: α , ι , υ

Exercise One

In this lessons' exercises we will be *transliterating*.

Transliteration is different than translating. You can think of transliteration as converting the sounds represented by letters in one language to the sounds of letters in another language. To help us learn the Greek alphabet, we will be using Greek letters to make English words. This allows one to get used to the Greek sounds using familiar words.

Example:

μηβι = "maybe." Notice that here the Eta stands for the 'ay' sound. The Iota is necessary because the Epsilon is a short vowel, and rarely (if ever) long. The Iota, however, sometimes makes the 'i' sound we hear in the word 'machine.'

It will just take practice and experience to figure out what sounds Greek letters can make. Strictly speaking, our purpose is to learn how to *read* Greek words, not speak them, so little attention will be spent on the sounds.

For this exercise, transliterate your name and the names of five other people you know. If your name is Tom, then the correct transliteration would be: τομ.

Exercise Two

Now that you have the idea—find the English equivalent of the following words:

δογ

χατ

ρυννινγ

χατσυπ

φιτνες

Now try some sentences:

θε φουντιν ις οφερφλωινγ.

μανι πιπλε χαν νοτ υνδερστανδ γρικ.

δου νοτ βιχομ ιντιμιδατεδ βι γρικ.

(Notice again that for 'greek' and 'become' you had to infer the 'ee' sound, as in 'machine')

Exercise Three

We are going to do more transliterating in this exercise.

Sit down at the computer with the word processor open. Change the font to 'symbol' or whatever the Greek letter font is for your program. Think about what you did this last weekend. Now, write out the story, in English, using the Greek alphabet. Make your story at least 50 words long and at most 100.

When you are finished, find a partner in your Greek class. Print off your story and give it to your partner, or email it to them. DO NOT SIMPLY WRITE THE STORY IN ENGLISH AND THEN SELECT IT ALL AND CHANGE THE FONT TO SYMBOL! Start in the 'symbol' font and work it out that way. Otherwise, what is the point of the exercise?

Exercise Four

We are going to have another exercise where we transliterate. This time, we will work from the Greek letters to the English word. Take the story from exercise three that you received from your partner and decode it back into the English words. Transliterate your partner's story back into English and submit it to your facilitator and compare it with the original. DO NOT SIMPLY CHANGE THE FONT BACK TO ENGLISH LETTERS!

Exercise Five

To help illustrate how easy Greek can be, take a look at these actual Greek words. Sound them out and see if you can guess what they mean.

βαπτισμα
σκορπιος
θεος
ανθροπος
θρονος
πατηρ

Exercise Six—BONUS

(for extra practice)

Find a favorite book. Open it to a full page and then either by hand or with the symbol font active, transliterate the English words into Greek letters. (For extra-extra practice, you can take someone else's Greek transliteration and convert it back into English). Then, read the passage aloud from the Greek letters for the English words.

Lesson Two

Nouns and Verbs

Once you have the letters of the language down, the next building block are the words. Nouns and Verbs form the majority of the words in most languages. It just so happens that in Greek it is a little easier to distinguish between nouns and verbs because the actual forms of them are different. A noun is formed differently than a verb.

Inflected Languages

Greek is an *inflected* language. As such, it is not like we are used to in our English language. However, many people are familiar with inflected languages if they've studied Spanish or German.

Even English is an *inflected* language to some degree. For example, you can distinguish between a singular noun and a plural noun because of the addition of the letter 's' after the noun. Example: 'Cat' is singular and 'Cats' is plural. That is an inflection. You don't need a whole new word to represent multiple cats because you just slap the 's' on it. (Although, if you think about it, there are times when we do. For example the plural of 'mouse' is not 'mouses' but rather a new word, 'mice')

Translating this English sentence, 'Your dog will run.' which takes four words, in the English, might only take two words in Greek. You can communicate 'Your dog' and 'will run' with just one word each in the Greek because possession is part of the noun form and tense is a part of the verb form. In some cases, even though word forms communicate all that is needed, helping words might still be provided.

First let us become familiar with nouns. (However, it should be noted that the same principles apply to adjectives!)

Examine these nouns:

λογος
αδελφος
αρτος
κυριος
πιστος
σταυρος

What do they all have in common? The ος ending.

λογ**ος**
αδελφ**ος**
αρτ**ος**
κυρι**ος**
πιστ**ος**
σταυρ**ος**

These are from the famed 'O' declension. Noun forms communicate the subject, possessive, indirect object, and direct object, and number, among other things. When the noun wants to change how many of a thing is being represented or whether or not it possesses something, the base of the word stays the same but the ending changes!

The full chart for a noun like λογος is:

The 'O' declension	Singular	Plural
Subject	λογ**ος**	λογ**οι**
Possessive	λογ**ου**	λογ**ων**
Indirect Object	λογ**ω**	λογ**οις**
Direct Object	λογ**ον**	λογ**ους**

Did you see how the ending changes depending on the number and case of the noun?

There is also the 'A' declension among nouns: θαλασσ**α**, εκκλησι**α**, εντολ**η**, ημερ**α**

The full chart of a noun in the 'A' declension, like ημερα is:

The 'A' declension	Singular	Plural
Subject	αγαπ**η**	αγαπ**αι**
Possessive	αγαπ**ης**	αγαπ**ων**
Indirect Object	αγαπ**η**	αγαπ**αις**
Direct Object	αγαπ**ην**	αγαπ**ας**

Teaching Tips:

1. In actual Greek, remember that there are accent and breathing marks for many Greek words. For our purposes, we can ignore them and when looking up a word it can be ignored as well. Obviously, higher levels of study will require an understanding of these marks.
2. The two charts above are just examples. There are other noun forms and there are exceptions everywhere! Students should be aware of this and warned not to expect hard and fast rules. We have very narrow goals in this course!

Now look at some verbs:

ακου**ω**
βλεπ**ω**
γραφ**ω**
κλεπτ**ω**

Verb forms communicate number, person, tense, and voice. Again, we will see that the ending of the word is what changes to reflect these attributes.

The full chart for a verb like βλεπω is:

	Singular	Plural
First person	βλεπ**ω** – I see	βλεπ**ομεν** – We see
Second person	βλεπ**εις** – You see	βλεπ**ετε** – You (all) see
Third person	βλεπ**ει** – He, She, It sees	βλεπ**ουσι** – They see

Teaching Tip: Though the endings seem to be multiplying we note that there is as yet only one place where there might be confusion: the first person singular of a verb and the singular indirect object of an 'O' declension noun where both end with 'ω.' Nothing but practice and experience can really resolve such issues. Eventually, with time and practice, students will get to know how different words behave.

Distribute Resource Two providing the charts comparing nouns and verbs and explain the following:

1. That Greek is an inflected language.
2. That nouns communicate number, whether it is the subject, possessive, indirect or direct object.
3. That verbs communicate person, number, tense (past, present, future, etc), and mood.
4. That many times a noun can be distinguished from a verb by comparing the endings.
5. That understanding a word's full meaning ultimately depends on being able to decode all of its parts, too.
6. The purchase of a Greek grammar and lexicons would be a good idea for dissecting complicated nouns and verb forms.

Teacher Tip: For more practice you can find more examples of Greek sentences for students to practice distinguishing between verbs and nouns.

Also, to take it to the next level, if you get your hands on a Greek grammar you can produce other 'declensions' and verb forms and show them to your students. Then, you will be able to spot even more verbs and nouns, having become aware of the different endings that are possible for each type.

This may sound formidable, but thankfully, though exceptions abound, there are also numerous patterns that are repeated.

NOTE:

The exercises for these and other lessons do not rely on memorization but if you really want to impress this information, you can easily create quizzes and tests by reproducing the empty charts and requiring students to fill them in by memory.

Nouns and Verbs
Resource Two

Nouns

Below are the charts for nouns with two different 'declensions.'

The full chart for a noun like λογος is:

The 'O' declension	Singular	Plural
Subject	λογος	λογοι
Possessive	λογου	λογων
Indirect Object	λογω	λογοις
Direct Object	λογον	λογους

The full chart of a noun like ημερα is:

The 'A' declension	Singular	Plural
Subject	αγαπη	αγαπαι
Possessive	αγαπης	αγαπων
Indirect Object	αγαπη	αγαπαις
Direct Object	αγαπην	αγαπας

Verbs

The full chart for a verb like βλεπω is:

	Singular	Plural
First person	βλεπω – I see	βλεπομεν – We see
Second person	βλεπεις – You see	βλεπετε – You (all) see
Third person	βλεπει – He, She, It sees	βλεπουσι – They see

Exercise One

Practice distinguishing between nouns and verbs. Put an N next to words that are nouns and a V next to words that are verbs. Make your best guesses.

αργον _____	παρακαλει _____
ακουετε _____	σταυροις _____
αδελφους _____	σταυρουτε _____
αγγενλοι_____	σωμα _____
ζωμεν _____	φερεις _____
ζωη _____	μισεω _____
λιθω _____	νιπτουσι _____
λεγου _____	ωφελει _____

Exercise Two

Below are five sentences from the Greek New Testament. You are not expected to be able to understand them. Your task is to go through and *circle every noun* and *underline every verb*. If you don't think it is either a noun or a verb—leave it alone!

οσοι δε ελαβον αυτον εδωκεν αυτοις εξουσιαν τεκνα θεου γενεσθαι τοις πιστευουσιν εις το ονομα αυτου (1:12)

λεγει αυτοις ερχεσθε και οψεσθε ηλθαν ουν και ειδαν που μενει και παρ αυτω εμειναν την ημεραν εκεινην ωρα ην ως δεκατη (1:39)

απεκριθη αυτω ναθαναηλ ραββι συ ει ο υιος του θεου συ βασιλευς ει του ισραηλ (1:49)

ουτως γαρ ηγαπησεν ο θεος τον κοσμον ωστε τον υιον τον μονογενη εδωκεν ινα πας ο πιστευων εις αυτον μη αποληται αλλ εχη ζωην αιωνιον (3:16)

ειπεν αυτοις ο ιησους εγω ειμι ο αρτος της ζωης ο ερχομενος προς εμε ου μη πειναση και ο πιστευων εις εμε ου μη διψηση πωποτε (6:35)

Exercise Three

(note to instructor: this exercise can also double as a quiz or a test)

For this exercise, use your resource sheet or rely on your memory to write in the correct endings for the two kinds of nouns and one kind of verb we have learned to this point.

The 'O' declension	Singular	Plural
Subject	λογ____	λογ____
Possessive	λογ____	λογ____
Indirect Object	λογ____	λογ____
Direct Object	λογ____	λογ____

The 'A' declension	Singular	Plural
Subject	αγαπ____	αγαπ____
Possessive	αγαπ____	αγαπ____
Indirect Object	αγαπ____	αγαπ____
Direct Object	αγαπ____	αγαπ____

	Singular	Plural
First person	βλεπ_____	βλεπ_____
Second person	βλεπ_____	βλεπ_____
Third person	βλεπ_____	βλεπ_____

Lesson Three

Using some Tools

We now have enough of a foundation to begin applying what we have learned. Since we are nowhere near having Greek memorized, we will have to use tools to make up the significant gaps. This lesson is meant to introduce several kinds of tools and familiarize students with them. We will work with the first three examples in this lesson. The remainder of the examples will be explored in Unit 2.

1. There is a Greek New Testament.

The Nestle-Aland editions are popular. These editions are helpful, too, because the textual apparatus is included. In other words, throughout the text, where manuscripts have disagreed or there are ambiguities or alternative readings, notes are provided. Consider it the ultimate in 'in depth' Bible study.

2. There are interlinears.

An interlinear Bible is one which puts the English text in one column and the Greek text in another column on the same page, side by side. Now, as you read the English you can glance over to see what the Greek is. Some interlinears only work off of the King James Version. Be sure to pay attention to what translation is being compared.

3. There are lexicons.

A lexicon is like a dictionary. A good lexicon will provide more than a definition and will provide other possible translations as well as other texts (both Biblical and extra-biblical) that make use of the word. The New Testament is written in 'koine' Greek so a lexicon keyed to that would be appropriate. ('Koine' means 'common' so 'koine Greek' means 'common Greek'). A classical Greek lexicon draws on the entire corpus of available Greek manuscripts from ancient times and will often include the New Testament. Both types of lexicons can be useful.

4. There are concordances.

The NIV Exhaustive Concordance is an especially useful tool. Not only is every word in the NIV cataloged, but the Greek (and Hebrew) words that were translated are cataloged, too. Not only can you conduct a word study of similar themes in the Bible in English, but you can also do a word study of the Greek words. For example, you can find all the places where the word 'love' is used in the Bible and identify all the places where the word 'agape' is used, and develop a comprehensive understanding of Biblical love. An Exhaustive Concordance, or a concordance keyed to the original language, is a very valuable tool for the student with limited knowledge of the original languages. In fact, theoretically, you wouldn't need any knowledge!

5. There are grammars and introduction to Greek texts.

A grammar book goes into vocabulary, sentence structure, accenting, rules, and exceptions of a language. Some Greek grammars are for advanced students, but others can be used by those just learning Greek, too. If one is trying to make sense of whole sentences or if one hopes to eventually be able to translate out of the Greek (or evaluate other translations) than purchasing some grammars would be essential. Most of the substance of this course is derived from material one can find in a grammar.

6. There are online tools.

The Internet has many tools available that used to be found only in books. Most of the above can be found online using a Google search. Quality varies and there are sometimes limitations. For example, the Nestle-Aland text can be found online because it is open source, but you may not find the manuscript notes. Still, if one doesn't want to invest a lot of money into a library of tools, the Internet can get you a long way.

7. Your local pastor.

In many denominations, pastors are trained in Greek and Hebrew in the course of their training to be pastors. Some use their training every week in the preparation for their sermons. Your pastor might not be able to translate on the fly anymore but he might be able to direct you in helpful directions.

The above material has been summarized as a resource sheet. Distribute that sheet and explain to them that:

1. Short of mastering Greek altogether they will have to use tools to help them.
2. There are a wide selection of tools to choose from.
3. Many tools are available on the Internet for free.

Based on the assumption that students have access to the Internet but haven't purchased all the suggested tools, the exercises will help them get familiar with some of the available online resources.

TOOLS FOR THE BIBLE STUDENT

Resource Three

The list below summarizes the kinds of tools you can use to help you access the original Greek behind your English translations.

1. a Greek New Testament.

A Greek New Testament is a New Testament completely in Greek and untranslated. It is very useful for seeing the whole passage in question and its context.

2. an interlinear.

An interlinear Bible is one which puts the English text in one column and the Greek text in another column on the same page, side by side. Now, as you read the English you can glance over to see what the Greek is.

3. lexicons.

A lexicon is like a dictionary. A good lexicon will provide more than a definition and will provide other possible translations as well as other texts (both Biblical and extra-biblical) that make use of the word. Many Greek New Testaments and grammars will have abbreviated lexicons in the back.

4. concordances.

A concordance lists the words used in the Bible and the passages where they are found. Some concordances are abbreviated while some catalog every word in the Bible. Some concordances are exhaustive—not only will they give you every word used in the Bible, but it will also tell you what the Greek and Hebrew words are, too. This is a very valuable tool for doing word studies.

5. grammars and introduction to Greek texts.

A grammar book goes into vocabulary, sentence structure, accenting, rules, and exceptions of a language. If one is trying to make sense of whole sentences or if one hopes to eventually be able to translate out of the Greek (or evaluate other translations) than purchasing some grammars would be essential.

6. online tools.

The Internet has many tools available that used to be found only in books. Most of the above can be found online using a Google search. Quality varies and there are sometimes limitations. Still, if one doesn't want to invest a lot of money into a library of tools, the Internet can get you a long way.

7. Your local pastor.

In many denominations, pastors are trained in Greek and Hebrew in the course of their training to be pastors. Some use their training every week in the preparation for their sermons. Your pastor might not be able to translate on the fly anymore but he might be able to direct you in helpful directions.

Exercise One

Using a Greek New Testament

The following link will take you to several sites with links to the Greek New Testament: http://www.ntgateway.com/greek-ntgateway/greek-new-testament-texts/

Decide what your favorite Bible verse from the New Testament is and browse to it from one of the links on that page. Copy it into a word processor document. You already know what it means, of course, but see how many of the words in the verse are words you've already learned. Make a list from the verse of the words you know and list their meanings. Then, circle the nouns and underline the verbs. Remember this exercise—you will return to it in later lessons.

Exercise Two

Using an Interlinear

A good online interlinear is located here: http://www.studylight.org/isb/

Think about your favorite passage from Exercise One. Use the link above to search for it. For example, if your favorite passage was John 3:16 you might either put John 3:16 directly into the search or you might put in the search word 'God so love' and selected 'New Testament.' You would eventually arrive at a page that looks like this:
http://www.studylight.org/isb/bible.cgi?query=joh+3:16&it=nas&ot=bhs&nt=na&sr=1

Now you should be able to see the English and Greek text right next to each other. You will be able to click on both the English and Greek words. Identify at least one word from your passage that you would like to learn more about. Click on the Greek word. Write down what that word is and what it means. Then, from the meanings provided, provide one insight into the text that you have gained that you wouldn't have had if you hadn't looked at the Greek word. (If the word you choose doesn't have much information, choose another word, or if your passage is too short maybe try another passage).

Share your findings with your facilitator and/or other students.

Exercise Three

Using a Concordance and Lexicon

Again, using your favorite passage, identify a word within it that you would like to perform a word study on. Note, most online concordances are 'public domain' so some of them are out of date.

To compensate for that, we will use the Interlinear/Concordance/Lexicon feature located here: http://bible.crosswalk.com/InterlinearBible/bible.cgi

Now, using this feature, find five other passages that use the same Greek word as the one you chose from your favorite passage. List those passages. Then, examine each to determine at least one new insight into your favorite text that you gained from looking at the other texts. For example, if you chose to look up the word 'love' from John 3:16 you would come to a page like this:
http://bible.crosswalk.com/Lexicons/Greek/grk.cgi?number=25&version=nas

On the right side you see a list of the books of the New Testament and all the instances that word is used in those books. From there you can browse the Greek and English of those Bible passages.

List your five passages you found that had the same Greek word in it and share your newly gained insight with your facilitator and/or fellow students.

Exercise Four

Using *All* the Tools

Identify your next favorite passage. Using all of the tools that you have learned how to use, investigate the Greek words in use in that passage. Use your Greek New Testament or an interlinear to find the actual Greek words behind your English translation. Use your lexicon to see what other possible translations there might have been for two or three of the words. Report your findings in a two to three paragraph essay.

Biblical Greek in A *Flash*

Unit 2

Who is this for? Those wishing to teach Greek... teachers, parents, homeschoolers, pastors, youth directors
What will be learned? Enough Greek to open up the New Testament and look up the words they find
Who will benefit? Anyone wanting to take their study of the Bible to the next level!

This is Unit 2 of the *Biblical Greek in a Flash* program. In the first unit, the alphabet was mastered, nouns and verbs were presented, and reference tools were introduced and utilized.

The purpose of this unit is to expand upon the first with the same narrow goal of enabling learners to find out what the Greek is behind their English text and use reference tools to come to a better understanding of what they are reading in the English. The purpose *is not* to become conversant in Greek or be able to translate passages out of the Greek into English.

It is assumed that the learner:

- knows the Greek alphabet
- is generally able to recognize and distinguish between nouns and verbs
- is able to navigate a Greek New Testament
- is able to look up Greek words in a Greek lexicon

At the end of this unit, students will:

- be better able to recognize and distinguish between nouns and verbs
- be able to recognize and distinguish between definite and indefinite articles
- be able to recognize and distinguish between pronouns
- have a very basic understanding of Greek grammar
- Know about fifty Greek words
- have a basic foundation for further study of the Greek language.

How long will it take?

Like Unit 1, the three lessons in Unit 2 can be spread out one lesson a week for three weeks or slow it down by repeating exercises or taking longer to do them and extend it to six weeks.

How old should the learner be?

The techniques used in Unit 1 have been employed with students as early as 7th grade. If your 7th grader can handle Unit 1 it is very likely they can handle Unit 2. However, since Unit 2 requires more memorization it might be necessary or wise to delay it until 8th grade. Use your discretion.

This program is an adaptation of the "Introduction to Biblical Greek" course provided by the Athanatos Online Apologetics Academy which is located at www.academyofapologetics.com. As such, this program makes use of widely available Internet resources and computer tools.

Lesson Four

Articles, Adjectives, Pronouns

An article would be 'a' or 'the.' In Greek, like English, these little words are all over the place.

Greek has one advantage over English, though: in Greek, the little words often have to 'agree' with the big words. Consider the *definite article* for example.

The definite article is essentially the word 'the' and accomplishes basically the same thing in Greek as it does in English.

Here is the chart for the 'O' declension noun compared with the 'O' declension definite article:

The 'O' declension	NOUNS		DEFINITE ARTICLES	
	Singular	Plural	Singular	Plural
Subject	λογο**ς**	λογ**οι**	**ο**	**οι**
Possessive	λογ**ου**	λογ**ων**	τ**ου**	τ**ων**
Indirect Object	λογ**ω**	λογ**οις**	τ**ω**	τ**οις**
Direct Object	λογ**ον**	λογ**ους**	τ**ον**	τ**ους**

You can clearly see that the endings for the definite articles match up with the noun endings. So, if you wanted to say 'the word' you would say 'ο λογος.'

We said that the Greek offers an advantage. It is this: in English it may be uncertain who the 'the' refers to but in Greek the 'the' will always match the thing it refers to! Thus, there is no ambiguity.

The same is true for adjectives and pronouns. They also *must* agree. So, if you wanted to say 'the good word' you would say 'ο αγαθος λογος.' If there was another noun in the sentence you would know that αγαθος modifies the word λογος and not the other noun because the endings for αγαθος and λογος agree. Also, in theory, word order is less important. You could put the definite article five words away from the noun it is modifying and you would still be able to match it up.

What about the *indefinite article*? That is the little word 'a' as in '*a* good word.' There is no indefinite article in the Greek language! When you see a noun unmodified with a definite article, it can be translated two different ways. For example:

λογος

can be translated as both 'a word' and 'word.' How does a translator decide? Context.

Before we go on, we need to mention another fact about Greek that is poorly reflected in the English language. Namely, Greek nouns have a 'gender.' It is not much different than Spanish. There are masculine, feminine, and neuter words.

What declension a noun follows depends on whether it is 'masculine' or 'feminine' or 'neuter.' While it is true that nouns ending with ος are typically masculine and nouns ending with α or η are typically feminine, there are too many exceptions to give hard and fast rules.   However, when you are trying to pick nouns out of a sentence you can often figure out whether it is masculine or feminine because of the form of the adjective or definite articles—because again, they must agree.

So, with that in mind, study the full article chart:

	MASCULINE	FEMININE	NEUTER
	Singular		
Subject	ο	η	το
Possessive	του	της	του
Indirect Object	τω	τη	τω
Direct Object	τον	την	το
	Plural		
Subject	οι	αι	τα
Possessive	των	των	των
Indirect Object	τοις	ταις	τοις
Direct Object	τους	τας	τα

If you compare that chart with the noun charts given in Lesson Two you will see the similarities. The above chart is for the definite article but the exact same principle is applied for adjectives, too. The only problem is that adjectives, even while they still *must* agree, do not always have the same endings. That is because a noun might be masculine but the adjective modifying it might have its *own form*. Fortunately, in many cases they do have the same endings, so for our purposes we are not going to reproduce a separate chart for adjectives. If anything, they'd follow the noun charts.

Pronouns, as you can guess, will have many of the same endings as the nouns and definite articles. Though there are some variations, that is indeed the case.

Below are the charts for the first, second, and third person personal pronouns.

First Person	Singular		Plural	
Subject	εγω	I	ημεις	we
Possessive	εμου / μου	my	ημων	our
Indirect Object	εμοι / μοι	(to) me	ημιν	(to) us
Direct Object	εμε / με	me	ημας	us

Second Person	Singular		Plural	
Subject	συ	you	υμεις	you (all)
Possessive	σου	your	υμων	your (all)
Indirect Object	σοι	(to) you	υμιν	(to) you (all)
Direct Object	σε	you	υμας	you (all)

Third Person	MASCULINE		FEMININE		NEUTER	
	Singular					
Subject	(αυτος)		(αυτη)		(αυτο)	
Possessive	αυτου	his	αυτης	her	αυτου	its
Indirect Object	αυτω	(to) him	αυτη	(to) her	αυτω	(to) it
Direct Object	αυτον	him	αυτην	her	αυτο	it
	Plural					
Subject	(αυτοι)		(αυται)		(αυτα)	
Possessive	αυτων	their	αυτων	their	αυτων	their
Indirect Object	αυτοις	(to) them	αυταις	(to) them	αυτοις	(to) them
Direct Object	αυτους	them	αυτας	them	αυτα	them

While the keen eye will have noted little exceptions here and there, the patterns are easy to spot. The principle to keep in mind is that pronouns, adjectives, and definite articles have to agree with the nouns they refer to. There are variations on that theme, but this is good enough for our purposes.

Distribute the charts to the students and explain to them that:

1. There is no indefinite article ('a').
2. The definite article must agree with the noun it modifies.
3. The adjective must agree with the noun it modifies.
4. The personal pronouns must agree with the noun they modify.
5. Exceptions and/or variations exist.
6. Nouns can be masculine, feminine, or neuter, and have different forms based on which they are.
7. The adjectives will often and the articles nearly always will have the same endings as the nouns they agree with.

Articles, Adjectives, Pronouns
Resource Four

Definite Article and Adjective Endings	MASCULINE	FEMININE	NEUTER
	Singular		
Subject	ο	η	το
Possessive	του	της	του
Indirect Object	τω	τη	τω
Direct Object	τον	την	το
	Plural		
Subject	οι	αι	τα
Possessive	των	των	των
Indirect Object	τοις	ταις	τοις
Direct Object	τους	τας	τα

Personal Pronoun Charts

First Person	Singular		Plural	
Subject	εγω	I	ημεις	we
Possessive	εμου / μου	my	ημων	our
Indirect Object	εμοι / μοι	(to) me	ημιν	(to) us
Direct Object	εμε / με	me	ημας	us

Second Person	Singular		Plural	
Subject	συ	you	υμεις	you (all)
Possessive	σου	your	υμων	your (all)
Indirect Object	σοι	(to) you	υμιν	(to) you (all)
Direct Object	σε	you	υμας	you (all)

Third Person	MASCULINE		FEMININE		NEUTER	
	Singular					
Subject	(αυτος)		(αυτη)		(αυτο)	
Possessive	αυτου	his	αυτης	her	αυτου	its
Indirect Object	αυτω	(to) him	αυτη	(to) her	αυτω	(to) it
Direct Object	αυτον	him	αυτην	her	αυτο	it
	Plural					
Subject	(αυτοι)		(αυται)		(αυτα)	
Possessive	αυτων	their	αυτων	their	αυτων	their
Indirect Object	αυτοις	(to) them	αυταις	(to) them	αυτοις	(to) them
Direct Object	αυτους	them	αυτας	them	αυτα	them

Exercise One

Practice identifying and distinguishing between pronouns and definite articles. In the table below, place a 'P' next to pronouns and 'A' next to the articles.

αυτους	_____	ο	_____
υμας	_____	ταις	_____
τα	_____	εγω	_____
ημεις	_____	σοι	_____
αι	_____	σε	_____
της	_____	το	_____

Exercise Two

Below are the same five sentences from Lesson Two, Exercise Two. This time, *circle the definite articles* and *underline the personal pronouns*. To the best of your ability, *draw lines connecting the articles with the nouns* they agree with.

οσοι δε ελαβον αυτον εδωκεν αυτοις εξουσιαν τεκνα θεου γενεσθαι τοις πιστευουσιν εις το ονομα αυτου (1:12)

λεγει αυτοις ερχεσθε και οψεσθε ηλθαν ουν και ειδαν που μενει και παρ αυτω εμειναν την ημεραν εκεινην ωρα ην ως δεκατη (1:39)

απεκριθη αυτω ναθαναηλ ραββι συ ει ο υιος του θεου συ βασιλευς ει του ισραηλ (1:49)

ουτως γαρ ηγαπησεν ο θεος τον κοσμον ωστε τον υιον τον μονογενη εδωκεν ινα πας ο πιστευων εις αυτον μη αποληται αλλ εχη ζωην αιωνιον (3:16)

ειπεν αυτοις ο ιησους εγω ειμι ο αρτος της ζωης ο ερχομενος προς εμε ου μη πειναση και ο πιστευων εις εμε ου μη διψησει πωποτε (6:35)

Exercise Three

This exercise is the same as the previous one, only there are five new sentences. Again, *circle the definite articles* and *underline the personal pronouns*. To the best of your ability, *draw lines connecting the articles with the nouns* they agree with.

εγω ειμι ο μαρτυρων περι εμαυτου και μαρτυρει περι εμου ο πεμψας με πατηρ (8:18)

ταυτην την παροιμιαν ειπεν αυτοις ο ιησους εκεινοι δε ουκ εγνωσαν τινα ην α ελαλει αυτοις (10:6)

εγω και ο πατηρ εν εσμεν (10:30)

ου περι τουτων δε ερωτω μονον αλλα και περι των πιστευοντων δια του λογου αυτων εις εμε (17:20)

απεκριθη θωμας και ειπεν αυτω ο κυριος μου και ο θεος μου (20:28)

Exercise Four

(note to instructor: this exercise can also double as a quiz or a test)

For this exercise, either from memory or in consultation with your charts, correctly fill in the blanks.

Definite Article and Adjective Endings	MASCULINE	FEMININE	NEUTER
	Singular		
Subject			
Possessive			
Indirect Object			
Direct Object			
	Plural		
Subject			
Possessive			
Indirect Object			
Direct Object			

Personal Pronoun Charts

First Person	Singular	Plural
Subject	I	we
Possessive	my	our
Indirect Object	(to) me	(to) us
Direct Object	me	us

Second Person	Singular	Plural
Subject	you	you (all)
Possessive	your	your (all)
Indirect Object	(to) you	(to) you (all)
Direct Object	you	you (all)

Third Person	MASCULINE	FEMININE	NEUTER
	Singular		
Subject			
Possessive	his	her	its
Indirect Object	(to) him	(to) her	(to) it
Direct Object	him	her	it
	Plural		
Subject			
Possessive	their	their	their
Indirect Object	(to) them	(to) them	(to) them
Direct Object	them	them	them

Lesson Five

Learning Some Words

The chief purpose of this course is to enable students to be able to find the Greek words 'beneath' the English ones they encounter in their Bible studies. Then, after they find the word they're looking for, they will be able to look the word up in a lexicon, or even find out other places where that same word is used. In theory, no vocabulary is needed at all to accomplish these goals. However, in practice, a mastery of at least some common and important words will make the process much easier.

Important Nouns:

God	θεως
Jesus	Ιησους
faith	πιστις
love	αγαπη
disciple	μαθητες
father	πατηρ
heart	καρδια
word	λογος
I am	ειμι
man	ανθρωπος
brother	αδελφος
Lord	κυριος
cross	σταυρος

Important Verbs:

I love	αγαπεω
I believe	πιστευω
say/said	λεγω/λεγει
I write	γραφω
I go	αγω
I hear	ακουω
I send	πεμπω
I see	βλεπω
I know	γνωσκω
I teach	διδασκω

Important Little Words:

this	τουτο
and/but	και
one	εις, μια, εν
into	εις
on	εν,επι
out of	εκ
from	απο
in	εν
with	συν
on the one hand	μεν
on the other hand	δε
and not	ουδε
not	ουκ / μη
because	οτι/γαρ
before	προ
when?	ποτε
where?	που
how?	πως
but (emphatic)	αλλα
Who/Which/What?	τις

The list above is obviously abbreviated—there is a whole language to learn if one wanted to pursue it! Depending on the level of study that you want to engage your students in, you can expand on this list by using the lists of vocabulary available in the back of a Greek New Testament or grammar. Note that we now have our first example of when an accent mark helps determine meaning. εις can either be 'one' or 'into.' The accent allows you to distinguish between them, though for our purposes, context comes in handy, too.

Learning Some Words

Resource Five

Use whatever technique you know to learn these words below. Using what you learned about the alphabet sounds, try to say the words aloud.

Important Nouns:

God	θεος
Jesus	Ιησους
faith	πιστις
love	αγαπη
disciple	μαθητες
father	πατηρ
heart	καρδια
word	λογος
I am	ειμι
man	ανθρωπος
brother	αδελφος
Lord	κυριος
cross	σταυρος

Important Verbs:

I love	αγαπεω
I believe	πιστευω
say/said	λεγω/λεγει
I write	γραφω
I go	αγω
I hear	ακουω
I send	πεμπω
I see	βλεπω
I know	γνωσκω
I teach	διδασκω

Important Little Words:

is	εστιν
this	τουτο
and/but	και
one	εἰς, μία, έν
into	εις
on	εν,επι
out of	εκ
from	απο
in	εν
with	συν
on the one hand	μεν
on the other hand	δε
and not	ουδε
not	ουκ / μη
because/for	οτι/γαρ
before	προ
when?	ποτε
where?	που
how?	πως
but (emphatic)	αλλα
Who/Which/What?	τις
was	ην

εις can either be 'one' or 'into.' We have not studied accents, but this would be one of the rare times when you need the accent to find out a word's meaning. For our purpose, use context, and with practice you will learn to tell the difference between the words.

Exercise One

Match up the Greek words with the English meaning by drawing lines connecting them:

(nouns and verbs only)

ειμι

μαθητες

God

Jesus   βλεπω

faith   πατηρ

love   θεος

disciple   πιστις

father   αγαπη

heart   ανθρωπος

word

I am   κυριος

man   αδελφος

brother   σταυρος

Lord   πεμπω

cross   γνωσκω

I love   καρδια

I believe   διδασκω

say/said   γραφω

I write   αγω

I go   Ιησους

I hear
                                            αγαπεω
I send   πιστευω

I see   λεγω/λεγει

I know
                                            λογος
I teach

                                            ακουω

Exercise Two

Match up the Greek words with the English meaning by drawing lines connecting them:

(verbs and 'little words' only)

is	αγαπεω
this	που
and/but	πως
one	αλλα
into	τις
on	εις
out of	μεν
from	εκ
in	απο
with	εν
on the one hand	τουτο
on the other hand	και
and not	εις, μια, εν
not	εν,επι
because/for	λεγω/λεγει
was	συν
when?	είς
where?	εστιν
how?	βλεπω
but (emphatic)	διδασκω
Who/Which/What?	δε
	ουδε
I love	ουκ / μη
I believe	οτι/γαρ
say/said	ην
I see	γνωσκω
I know	ποτε
I teach	πιστευω

Exercise Three

Match up the Greek words with the English meaning by drawing lines connecting them:

(Selected from All)

λογος

word	ειμι
I am	δε
on the one hand	αγαπεω
I love	ην
I believe	
say/said	πιστευω
is	λεγω/λεγει
this	εστιν
and/but	τουτο
God	και
Jesus	
faith	γνωσκω
love	θεος
I know	Ιησους
Lord	πιστις
not	αγαπη
because/for	ουκ / μη
out of	οτι/γαρ
from	κυριος
was	εκ
	απο

Exercise Four

From what you have learned so far, see if you can figure out what these passages from the New Testament say. Hint: κοσμος = world.

Passage 1:
εν αρχη ην ο λογος και ο λογος ην προς τον θεον και θεος ην ο λογος

Passage 2:
ουτως γαρ ηγαπησεν ο θεος τον κοσμον ωστε τον υιον τον μονογενη εδωκεν ινα πας ο πιστευων εις αυτον μη

αποληται αλλ εχη ζωην αιωνιον

Passage 3:
ειπεν αυτοις ο ιησους εγω ειμι ο αρτος της ζωης ο ερχομενος προς εμε ου μη πειναση και ο πιστευων εις εμε ου

μη διψησει πωποτε

Passage 4:
οταν εν τω κοσμω ω φως ειμι του κοσμου

Passage 5:
καθως ηγαπησεν με ο πατηρ καγω υμας ηγαπησα μεινατε εν τη αγαπη τη εμη

Exercise Five

(note to instructor: this exercise can also double as a quiz or a test)

In this vocabulary exercise, recall from memory the meanings of the following Greek words. Write the meanings next to the Greek words.

εις, εν	Ιησους
ακουω	πιστις
πεμπω	καρδια
βλεπω	λογος
γνωσκω	και
διδασκω	ειμι
λεγω/λεγει	ανθρωπος
γραφω	αδελφος
προ	κυριος
ποτε	σταυρος
που	αγαπη
αγω	μαθητες
εστιν	πατηρ
τουτο	αγαπεω
θεος	πιστευω
πως	εἰς
δε	εν,επι
ουδε	οτι
ουκ	ην
τις	αλλα
εκ	απο
συν	έν
μεν	μία
γαρ	μη

Lesson Six

Verb Tenses and More Practice with Resource Tools

In this lesson verb forms designating tenses (past tense, future tense, etc) will be introduced and more opportunity to investigate specific Bible passages using what has been learned, helped by reference tools, will be given. Please distribute Resource Three from Unit 1 if these have been misplaced.

Verb Tenses:

It was explained that verbs communicate number, person, etc, and *tense*. Because tense is important and because the Greek changes the very form of the word to reflect tense, some helpful hints here are appropriate.

In the English, one might say "He will go" but in the Greek, all three words can be communicated with just one word! We will deal with just two tenses—the past tense (aorist) and future tense. There are numerous other tenses, but the present, past, and future tenses are the most common, and fortunately, the easiest to recognize. To this point we have covered present tense forms.

Past Tense:

Generally speaking, a verb is put into past tense simply by putting an epsilon (ε) in front of it. The verb endings remain more or less the same. Because of the addition of the epsilon, the main word will sometimes change, though, contracting or expanding so that it sounds better coming out of the mouth.

Consider this verb chart for the *present tense* form for the word λειπω (I leave):

PRESENT TENSE	Singular	Plural
First person	λειπ**ω** – I leave	λειπ**ομεν** – We leave
Second person	λειπ**εις** – You leave	λειπ**ετε** – You (all) leave
Third person	λειπ**ει** – He, She, It leaves	λειπ**ουσι** – They leave

Now, here is the *past tense form* for the word λειπω:

PAST TENSE	Singular	Plural
First person	**ε**λιπ**ον** – I left	**ε**λιπ**ομεν** – We left
Second person	**ε**λιπ**ες** – You left	**ε**λιπ**ετε** – You (all) left
Third person	**ε**λιπ**ε** – He, She, It left	**ε**λιπ**ον** – They left

As you can see, there are remarkable similarities between the endings of the verb. The dead give away that you are dealing with a past tense word is the inclusion of the epsilon.

Future Tense:

The future tense has a 'dead give away' as well. Instead of adding a letter to the beginning of the word, though, it adds a letter to the beginning of our ending. That letter is the sigma (σ/ς). This can get a little tricky because in the Greek, when a π and an σ are together, the Greek speaker would just prefer to combine the sound into the letter ψ (the 'ps' sound). This is the case with our chosen example of λειπω, but it is essentially just adding the sigma. Observe:

PRESENT TENSE	Singular	Plural
First person	λειπ**ω** – I leave	λειπ**ομεν** – We leave
Second person	λειπ**εις** – You leave	λειπ**ετε** – You (all) leave
Third person	λειπ**ει** – He, She, It leaves	λειπ**ουσι** – They leave

Now, here is the *future tense form* for the word λειπω:

FUTURE TENSE	Singular	Plural
First person	λειψ**ω** – I will leave	λειψ**ομεν** – We will leave
Second person	λειψ**εις** – You will leave	λειψ**ετε** – You (all) will leave
Third person	λειψ**ει** – He, She, It will leave	λειψ**ουσι** – They will leave

The future tense endings can be thought of as σω, σεις, σει, σομεν, σετε, and σουσι.

The pattern generally holds.

The reason why it is important for our purposes to know that these changes happen is because we are focusing so much on being able to look up a word. In order to do that, you have to find out what the root word really is. If you see the epsilon you may guess that you are dealing with a past tense verb but if there is elision (http://en.wikipedia.org/wiki/Elision) you may not notice and therefore fail to identify the word in question. Similarly, though the sigma is easy to spot, it may change into a whole new letter, and again, one might fail to identify the exact word.

Obviously, if one is trying to determine what the word really means, then knowing its tense is necessary. If you come across ελιπες, it doesn't simply mean 'he leaves'—it means 'he left' and that makes a big difference! Here is where a Greek grammar becomes very important, even if online tools can be helpful. There are numerous verb forms and tenses. Even after you identify the right form, tense, mood, voice, etc, you have to know what they all mean! Your grammar can be a big help!

For this lesson, explain that:
7. In Greek, the verb contains the time/tense, unlike in English.
8. The Greek verb changes in regular patterns to reflect past, present, future tenses, etc.
9. There are exceptions to those patterns for a variety of reasons.
10. The past tense typically adds an epsilon to the front of the word.
11. The future tense typically adds a sigma to the front of the verb ending.

Present, Past, Future Tense
Resource Six

Consider this verb chart for the *present tense* form for the word λειπω (I leave):

PRESENT TENSE	Singular	Plural
First person	λειπ**ω** – I leave	λειπ**ομεν** – We leave
Second person	λειπ**εις** – You leave	λειπ**ετε** – You (all) leave
Third person	λειπ**ει** – He, She, It leaves	λειπ**ουσι** – They leave

Now, here is the *past tense form* for the word λειπω:

PAST TENSE	Singular	Plural
First person	**ε**λιπ**ον** – I left	**ε**λιπ**ομεν** – We left
Second person	**ε**λιπ**ες** – You left	**ε**λιπ**ετε** – You (all) left
Third person	**ε**λιπ**ε** – He, She, It left	**ε**λιπ**ον** – They left

Now, here is the *future tense form* for the word λειπω:

FUTURE TENSE	Singular	Plural
First person	λει**ψω** – I will leave	λει**ψομεν** – We will leave
Second person	λει**ψεις** – You will leave	λει**ψετε** – You (all) will leave
Third person	λει**ψει** – He, She, It will leaves	λει**ψουσι** – They will leave

The general rule is that to put a verb into past tense, you add the epsilon (ε) at the front of the word.

To put a verb into future tense, you add a sigma (σ). When a π and an σ are together the Greek combines them into one letter, the ψ, which is seen in the case of the future tense λειπω.

The future tense endings can be thought of as σω, σεις, σει, σομεν, σετε, and σουσι.

Exercise One

Look at the words below and determine what tense they are in. Put a 'Pre' for 'present' tense, a 'P' for 'past' tense, and a 'F' for 'future' tense next to them.

ελιπον   λειπεις   λυω   ελυσατε   λυσει   λυσετε   λειψουσι   εδηλουν   τιμησω

Exercise Two

Below are five more sentences.   Identify the verbs and then do your best to determine their tense for each. For each sentence, circle all the words you think are verbs, even if you don't think you've learned the tense yet. For those that are present, past, or future tense, say which tense you think the word is.

οσοι δε ελαβον αυτον εδωκεν αυτοις εξουσιαν τεκνα θεου γενεσθαι τοις πιστευουσιν εις το ονομα αυτου (1:12)

λεγει αυτοις ερχεσθε και οψεσθε ηλθαν ουν και ειδαν που μενει και παρ αυτω εμειναν την ημεραν εκεινην ωρα ην ως δεκατη (1:39)

ουτως γαρ ηγαπησεν ο θεος τον κοσμον ωστε τον υιον τον μονογενη εδωκεν ινα πας ο πιστευων εις αυτον μη αποληται αλλ εχη ζωην αιωνιον (3:16)

ειπεν αυτοις ο ιησους εγω ειμι ο αρτος της ζωης ο ερχομενος προς εμε ου μη πειναση και ο πιστευων εις εμε ου μη διψησει πωποτε (6:35)

εγω ειμι ο μαρτυρων περι εμαυτου και μαρτυρει περι εμου ο πεμψας με πατηρ (8:18)

Exercise Three

Correct your work! If you haven't figured it out already, all of the sentences we've worked with have been from the book of John. Take your results from Exercise Two and look up the passages in your English translation of John and see if you caught all the verbs. Then, see how well you caught present, past, and future tensed verbs. What tense are the remaining ones? Guess.

Exercise Four

(note to instructor: this exercise can also double as a quiz or a test)

Re-create the verb chart for the *present tense* form for the word λειπω (I leave):

PRESENT TENSE	Singular	Plural
First person	λειπ_____	λειπ_____
Second person	λειπ_____	λειπ_____
Third person	λειπ_____	λειπ_____

Re-create the *past tense form* for the word λειπω:

PAST TENSE	Singular	Plural
First person	__λιπ_____	__λιπ_____
Second person	__λιπ_____	__λιπ_____
Third person	__λιπ_____	__λιπ_____

Re-create the *future tense form* for the word λειπω:

FUTURE TENSE	Singular	Plural
First person	λει_____	λει_____
Second person	λει_____	λει_____
Third person	λει_____	λει_____

Exercise Five

Put it all Together

As your final project for the course, we will repeat Lesson Three, Exercise Four, with yet another favorite passage from the Bible. Below is that Lesson:

Using *All* the Tools

Identify your next favorite passage. Using all of the tools that you have learned how to use, investigate the Greek words in use in that passage. Use your Greek New Testament or an interlinear to find the actual Greek words behind your English translation. Use your lexicon to see what other possible translations there might have been for two or three of the words. Report your findings in a two to three paragraph essay.

Exchange your essay with another participant and talk about what you learned.

Conclusion

In general, this series has avoided using technical lingo whenever possible. The instructor is encouraged to pick up a Greek grammar so that he has the ability to track down the technical terms to make future study easier. For example, the term for 'possessive' which we have been using for the nouns is actually called the 'genitive case.' You'll find more information by looking up 'genitive case' than you will 'possessive.'

The techniques used in this course have been designed to give a working knowledge, not a translator's knowledge, of the Greek language. Many of the techniques have been employed for students as young as 7th grade and many of the same strategies have been employed for collegiate level basic Greek courses. Because of the power of transliteration and how many cognates there are (Greek and English words that sound alike and also mean about the same thing), a rudimentary knowledge of Greek is accessible to a variety of age groups.

It is strongly encouraged that the course instructor spend some time learning Greek themselves, including putting themselves through this very course, prior to teaching it.